AND FIVE, SIX, SEVEN, EIGHT!

Also by Kurt Erkan

Novel
Heaven Must Be Like This

AND FIVE, SIX, SEVEN, EIGHT!

KURT ERKAN

HETSOFF

ISBN: 978-3-00-045357-1

eISBN: 978-3-00-045358-8

Editor: Jennifer Geacone-Cruz

Cover design: River Raid

Book design: Virginie Lamoureux

Printed by CreateSpace, An Amazon.com Company

First paperback edition

First published in 2014

www.hetsoff.com

For my wife

REVERIE

Whenever I see you around,
Questions conquer my mind.
The first ones are; not quite tempting enough
Answers don't fool me — they're not necessary
But, a few steps close
A mounting pressure builds inside
That I can't hold in anymore,
It reaches my lips, moves them up and down
Then from side to side; no, not a smile
My voice says, "Did you learn to love, yet?"
I break into two for a moment.
Half of me facing you,
The other walks a few meters right
I watch our faces from the distance
An unexpected wind brushes by us.
Empty looks, no words to explain.
A plane full of memories takes off again.

Reverie

Indeed, I haven't seen you for a while,
You were, in my dreams, always alive
With answers worth listening to,
A tune singing on a familiar feeling
Slightly convincing me of love

GREEN

It's as if I know you from the past
From somewhere with rainy weather
Yet full of hope
In a place where all the letters are written
Then signed, sealed and delivered
Nobody is sure, whether they are read
Will those words ever be said
Out loud again?

It's as if you're talking, right next to me
You now wear glasses
And a shiny ponytail
You are speaking a language,
I don't understand
But with an air of calmness

Your words sound as if like

You're not going to leave,
Soon
It's as if it's not
Forbidden to trust
One another
Or the love behind us
In a place where I can't breathe in your words,
But your familiar perfume.
Do you still wear it?
Do you think of me taking it off?

But I see your eyes
While you're speaking words in disguise
They never change, never change in time
And I understand green
Since the beginning of our time.

SEASONS

Hey guys!
Not to be rude but
Can I ask, who needs you indeed?
I don't want to be mean, simply
What do you mean for this miserable mankind
Hey Summer, darlin'
Why don't you show us some more lightning
If I were you I'd try striking
Us—you can do it, too
On the flipside, Mr Winter
All I do in this life
Is to listen to those saying
"You have to win! Tear them apart!"
But nobody asks me,
Do I even want to?
Do I even have the power?
A bit of this, a bit of that

Autumn, with that wide swath of colors
On her lap
Dancing on our emotions
Oh damn, isn't this much enough to suffer
Stories, movies, memories
Left behind, forgotten dreams
I was just about to say, I'm done
All of a sudden Spring comes along
This time, dear, what now?
Can't you make a deal with the sun above
The good life stays there, silent
Like an alluring elixir in a bowl
I approach and just when I take a sip,
Ring the bells of the whole universe
Let them all know that
Time passes anyway.
Who needs seasons to accompany
This cloudy, dark melancholy
We stand, breathe and decay
Every second we live today
The best part is that
We don't need any of these seasons

To be there
To be happy and hopeful
And afterwards, dead.

FRENCH

Would you like to play a game;
Say your words in French then
Should I care if you can speak that or not
Listen, listen to the girl singing
Soft, delicate, so fragile
Like you can feel pity for her
In this wild world, alone
All she has are the words, honey
Throw your words to me
Tell me your stories that
I wasn't a part of
Life starts now, with you
Do you feel it
Do you care if I feel or not
Life is so selfish, honey
Keeps moving along
Makes the sun turn around, dizzy

Doesn't care if we love or not
Love me, keep the bliss for yourself
Love me, keep making me myself
Love me.

LAST CHANCE

Bit by bit
I fall into the stirred deep
Maybe you're going to be around
This afternoon, or the next
Taking Charlie out to the park
For him to poop in joy
Running round and round
Come save me while you have time
At least while you still can try
Today, this-day or that-ur-day
Will it matter much?
I am there somehow
To have and to hold, and it goes on
Don't we all need to be
A little fragment of a bond
Strong one; quite enduring
It brings the buzz we long for

All that jazz of an ordinary afternoon
All those tiny faults we are supposed to fix
If we are lucky enough
A surprise visit from the lost sun
Put a song on top of it, singing on the radio
If we still even own one
Everything changes with the morning light
Some days it wakes us with a sweet smell,
Fusion of the coffee you make and
The savory scent of your neck.
But the same light sometimes
Breaks our hearts, as we open our eyes
Why does he need to do that,
Can't we leave all that behind,
Can't we all forget and hide,
And start again
Here, time wakes another tide
Come, hold my hand

SHORTER STORY

You give me the strength to outdo
Monday mornings
Even without being by my side
If we just rent a dream
From the world's best dreamer—
Probably a kid somewhere—
Without a toy to travel in through
Time and space
And picture us together
Heading to open sea from a lonely bench
On the Oslo shore
City behind us, left alone
Sea in front of my eyes, calm and inviting
No memories, no looks
Just a connecting of minds between both of us
You and me, simply
Like a page from a short story

Wouldn't it?

TUNE

A quiet room
A sea of voices within
An orchestra playing
Obey the maestro
And let the songs drill into your heart

If you're not willing to tell everything
You should meet someone who
Likes to deal in riddles
From memories, and the current moment
Shadows playing a movie on the wall
Night and dark around
But you're not alone
You are with yourself
With your best friend

All through the nothingness

Without seeing purely
I touch the walls which stand apart
I walk, not knowing where it'll lead
Hoping that it leads to you

Our past times
Tied to a rope
Pulled from us
To a cemetery of
Forgotten seconds
Be my first
Stay my thirst

FLAMES

If I bribe the clouds
Or learn a bit of magic somehow
Will it be enough to make a fresh, delicate,
delicious rain
To wash out your occupied cabinets
That are kept reserved in your heart
Or I run to you at that very moment
Under that misty spell
Will it tear down my regrets, mistakes
Or at least my pain.

If it doesn't heal us anyhow,
Let us burn anyway
At least we can hope that the tiny drops
After drops, after drops
May touch the face of a kid
Who doesn't know anything about love

But soak him with it, at the beginning
Of his life
Although he may never heal again

OXYGEN

Wake up, leave the burning bed behind
Wrap yourself with the morning sun
If it's winter time
Bathe with the sacred mist
If it's not the season of
Beautiful dark mornings
Pray that it's going to be winter soon
Don't let the summer joy
Outdo our unique sorrow
Let it stay, let it conquer
Let it make you see
That life is not that shallow.
Heal yourself with the chill
At a quiet corner under a winter shadow
If you can find one
If you can find yourself
Then look for a soul,

↘ Oxygen

Touch
See
Listen.
You don't need to talk
Look in the eyes and breathe in the moment
And abandon the question of
Why are we alive

LAUNDROMAT

Can't we just pretend
Even if only for now — on a miserable
November night
That we've met at a laundromat
A regular and decent Tuesday afternoon,
When sun was going down — if we could
convince him,
With a last touch on your hair, to make it
Shine more, just in case you needed to
Attract more
Souls who were in need of a washing

Were you always like this?
This delicate, this beautiful and mostly
This merciless?
Or, is this for me, especially
I have an idea. After the washing

Let's go to the market where
Morning joy is sold
To the tiny birds — at a wholesale price
We'll chase that a few bucks, of course

Sleep rains on me heavily
The joy that I've found in the morning
Has slipped out of my hand;
On the ground now, under
Hectic big city feet
Metropolitan rush
Everybody has a crush
Dead now, the joy, remember?

Are you happy
Do you want to see the corpse
Lying still, alone and naked
No soul, just the body
Of mourning joy

Pray for a cloud to come over
(She should stop posing for phones)

Come down to you to
Wash the last bits of smiles you once had
She's a good friend; she'll do it
Trust me
The coalition of the mother nature
Connected to your heart
Now, it's your turn to
Plug that into your mind

Faces will stare at a cold laundromat
On an ugly laundry day
Do you still care?
Be stingy with your words, honey
Wise and shine
As you always do
And I miss you
As I always do

You go out alone.

LAKES

Anyone can,
You know, dream
Moonlight over a lake of dreams
Until life strikes out
At our backs,
Defenceless mechanisms
That we were born with
A lifetime of deep pleasures
Until when — or what — we can endure
God knows
(Confess; now you got it)

In the end, these days must come and go
To the place where they belong
Sun, up and down, a bit circular
Moon, bright and dim, somehow friendlier
Breathe in, breathe out

Just to pull ourselves together

We need to reach the source
That emits the light
Within and without
Life is easy, if you
Trace the illuminant
A favorable delight
If you like

Repeat
Breathe in, breathe out
And walk inside.

LINES

Late autumn, noonish, Tuesday
We were on a bridge, in a dark Paris
Barely knew each other — which was nice
You were in black heels, stockings and a skirt
Like a November night next to me
Your hair was the daylight of that
Beautiful scenery
And I was the knight of the scenario
Opened its doors wide
Looks were sharper than touches
Stories were tastier than tongues
Minutes became frozen with our heat, however
Time had done its duty,
Brought the end so quickly
Or wait, did you instead say "It wasn't love?"
What do we have now on our hands
A slight longing maybe,

Memories of a distant scent
And an unforgotten flesh
Isn't it strange that we still live
On the same planet
But behave as if each other were invaders
From another galaxy
On a mission to conquer
An ordinary life, on an ordinary day
In an extraordinary way
Destinies cross, amplify lives
Then separate, with only a trace
Just like a faint tune
In a melody that we hear
Again and again

FRAGILE

If some day a very wise man
Comes across these lines, or
Some others that I've written
And decides to analyse how
Psychopathic, or wishful, or
A phony romantic, or a fetishistic
For a lot of things he'd think;
Absurd and foolish
Then again, nothing will change
No matter what
This pen will be elevated somehow
Fly over my desk, or over the coffee table
Of some strangers
And land in my hand,
Connect with my mind
And will write recklessly, again.
This is the only truth and

Remedy I know.
This is how I define
Being lucky.
Then that fortunate self,
After a deep breath inside,
Will let all those chemicals
Do their business instead.
Behind him, while he reacts
To the cruelty of the world
Some people, (not all)
Will pray silently
"Please, don't fall, please don't fall"
Maybe.
This could be...

NAVY BLUE

Who had promised you a red boat?
I mean, why not white, why red to you
Or, it could have been blue
Like handsome navy men around
They all wear blue, stuck on with clichéd glue
You fool, you forget some rules to remember
Or do you already think that they are dead?
Dreams are back in sleep

You are tie-red
Wake up, but no make-up today
For the sake of morning sun
Or you may take it as a sacrifice
Of yesterday's ruin
Miss the rest, everything you left behind
Either a mistake, or a cause to be proud

Like a kid rejecting sleep
You abandon me — never wanted to
Walk towards us
If the nightingale we heard back then
Could play a violin like he's deeply hurt
Would you love him more
Instead of me
With all those touchy whines of the instrument
With all that sorrow I tried to mean
When I was in your dream
Which you named "Gale in a mare"
No nights to remember
Time to wake up
Somebody wake me up.

HUNTER

I continuously hunt down words
They fly in groups like migrating birds
No restrictions for us — hunters
Neither season nor place
We hunt for hearts these days
They are hungry for food, dear
Food for our lasting aches
In that muscle that beats and contracts
Tired for only a day in life
Governments do something!
Can't we have days off for these breakable fists

My disappointments drip page by page
All alone I stare
Nothing more anybody can do
Than to accept and bow to life
For the merciless sorrow it brings

Every morning, every dawn
No, not you indeed, dear life
But a poison called expectation
Running in our blood
Stream by stream hear the notes of the moment
Time is playing for you

Take off the protective layer of your soul
Face the day
Take courage in the hunters working for you
Not to be lost in the jungle
Not to be broken
In the big city
Not to be defeated
By the grey
Of the new day

OWNER OF LIES

Will you tidy up your desk
Open a new document,
Or a newly bought notebook
And write a memoir one day?
What would you tell
All the minutes you've murdered?
As your digital watch ticks and tocks
While time takes a piece from all of us
What would you think
About the days been spent
And the happiness you've had inside?

Every now and then,
The human mind likes to play games
Invent things and some nice surprises
That have never really been lived
Making believe

The things we've never forgotten indeed
Where do these lies come from?
Do they like visitors?
Can we pick them without permission?
Or, is it only for proprietors
Of soul.

Please ask these questions to your memories
During your research
For the aforementioned memoir

STAIN ON BRAIN

Now and then, some literary movements
That's off topic now, sorry...
Or, some pseudo-important political issues —
Previously planned, lately staged
This-and-that columns in the last
New Yorker issue,
Issues of everyday life, like
Sun going up – rising, sun going down – setting
My risen soul against the ordinary
Never understands me,
Never convinces to be settled
We look for some movements to lose ourselves to
— Me and my risen soul
We come together to live; why?
We don't know.
We read a lot, asked a lot, thought a hell of a lot...
Nothing. Comes. Up. Except sun!

Some movements oh-so-very...
Unimportant simply.
She has a shower, then dries her hair
08:24 on a Thursday morning at the corner of
50th and 7th
A surprise cousin of the sun – a gentle breeze
Ruffles her hair for a slow second
With a velvet movement
What do we do?
Do we have consciousness then,
Or, other thoughts – God damn!
Or just "now," and the hair-flow?
Locked in time.
Looked in hype.
That is all we can see.

ST GERMAIN

It becomes really impossible these days
To count the birds flying over us
In big cities – whether you live there or visit
That's a problem Miss, don't you think?
Can't you see how much this takes away from us
From lives, short-lived daydreams?
It isn't important, you think
Because we got twitter now
In every city, in every town

Forget all these superficial attentions
Focus on a flower shop
On Boulevard Saint-Germain
Have a coffee on the way, from the most
Snobbish hand gesture the world has ever seen
You may even ask the lady with the faux fur coat
And the high heels that tap on the road

"Where did you hide this beauty
That you don't show the world
On your photographs?"
If you're lucky she'll answer you between
A tic-toc and a tap-tap
"I know, I know, I don't show what I've got
As often as I should."
Know yourself, it is the virtue

You bring me emotions wherever I go
Like a bouquet of flowers from a distant life
Wasn't I living before?
Wasn't I breathing the passing air-flow
As often as I should?
Colourful beauties smelling questions
Not belonging here
Not belonging today
An older man leans down and
Whispers in my ear
"Sinful roses from the garden of hell."
Hours pass every day
Do we care about that,

↘ *St Germain*

Or the roses in our hand?

DRUM ROLL

How hard it is to sharpen
A numb mind which doesn't know
Where it's going
Although how I've wished it to be otherwise
To be enlightened
Seeing oneself lacking knowledge
"Shame on me" kind of thoughts
Than to crave your way forward
Lessons learned, you'll say
How the life, the world
The trees on the sidelines of the roads
That lead to
Our dreams, if not dream-like moments
With an ordinary friend
Or an extraordinary foe
Or a surprise lover, if you'd like
Would be different than they all are now

How meaningless that darker cloud on the left is
To you
Or, the less crowded cafe
With the better coffee
Nobody knows but you
Only then, we could all affect each other
For the better
That the world could be nicer
With that detached normality of theirs,
Leaves us breathless.
And beauty within regularity
It might be that simple,
To be happy.
If only
We could see.

Maybe we could do that
Eventually a space will open up
In case you haven't known it
By now.

THAT DANCE

You always,
Always, always leave that red stain
On your coffee cup.
Left, leaving and going to leave
All ways.
Then do you still want me to forget?
Do we have our personal nuclear bombs
With us, ready?
Always, always
When are we going to... You know...
We'll see.
Okay.

I always dreamed of you as a dancer
With all those turns and
Clear-cut stances
To dance me away

From this cruel, cruel world
To the place that... Is not earth.
How about the bomb?
Are we going to use it?
Not yet. Wait.
Okay.

An unknown smile
Like a birthday present
For a Cancer on a December
Day — and they don't know.
Dark morning, misty air
Do you know how easy it sometimes is
To make me happy?
Sure you do.
Always. All ways.
A brain with a beautiful face
Are we going to use it —
The bomb?
If you'd like.
If it's the time.

No need to wait, then.
Everybody's going to leave
Before they lie
Down, before dawn.

Now, it's time!
On your marks!
And five, six, seven, eight!

FLYING SKIRTS

Good music, that vibe all around
Some faces we know, some new
Souls never met before
As fresh as a sin never made.
Liquid surprise ready for us
No parents home today, isn't that enough?

Underwater silence all around me
Suddenly; never saw it coming
How about you?
What do you see,
In your world, if hasn't yet become a lucid dream
With the one you've mentioned
At a small party; do you recall?
In a city you don't know well —
Well, that's the good part, we like that —
But, well enough?

To leave someone you love behind
Blindly, easily
As if winter was an early bird returning this year.
It was the night, you remember?
That you said, you couldn't
Sleep well.

Look, I have an idea.
Why don't we make today
Like one of those old times,
Never-minding at its best
Like when we think that
The flying skirts are the
Most beautiful things in the world.
Then we may
Let the rest follow.

DOCTOR

Then with an air of clumsiness
About the way it happens
Or, the way we see it
Not important,
The absoluteness of things
Doesn't matter to anybody
We look for some happiness
In the most unusual pieces of soul

The doctor is doubtful of
The skills necessary
To improve the healing capacity
In order to get rid of you
And I had no choice but to tell him
I need to write
Hey, holy remedy
Am I the peculiar one

Or, is he?

You can do those things to me
Like a gifted sculptor,
I crave your image in my mind;
Sometimes the flow of your curls
Is it a trap for me:
Left that way after a noon shower
Maybe on a day during a mid-summer
With the wind coming to help.
Here, a tattoo in my memory,
You sometimes sit on the windowsill
To read a couple of pages;
While this scene makes me put down
Nearly a million pages
With your statue and the tattoo.

Those visiting hours pass so quick
They take your image mercilessly
Alone

A LITTLE LEFT

I count the bricks on my way back
Black, dark brown and red
On the walls, guiding my way
In a friendlier way, I suppose.
I thought of them as small lockers
Where your scent confined within
Diffused in front of me
With every new step I take
A mild breeze blows, but no destruction
Hair all around waved, but no boats on heads
Black, dark brown and red
Hands go up, make it tidier
Be sure that everything's in place
A little left, the rest to the back
Anxious thoughts... under that, too
A little left, the rest
Always back

In the days.
Black, dark brown and red.

JUPITER

This time, how about making a change
And keeping your promise
Like a buried melody.
When I walk alone, all by myself
I might hear your tune
On a newly born
Jasmine blossom along my way.
Her smell, your touch

I move my feet on a deserted sidewalk
With a million bodies hurrying along
Each and every one of them
Carrying a delicate urban soul

Under a gold street light
With a couple of silver star lights,
Fusion in illumination

↘ Jupiter

A vague midnight shadow by my heart

I said change, right?
Let's start all over;
Spread a black canvas over us
Like we're lost in outer space
Nobody could see
We're wild and naked underneath
They just observe Jupiter next to us
With their tiny telescopes for beginners
They aren't going to know.
But for only one soul,
Is it you?

SILENT CRY

Tonight in Berlin
There was an apartment on a second floor
With a tawny light turned on inside
It seems like
There's a yellow fair gathering
Out of hope, maybe
A party, it could be
Laughter, flirting ladies and gentlemen
No earthly anxiety
Everything's in order.

But, NO!
There was a cry in silence on the window
Written in black capital letters
It says "HELP!"
Yes, with an exclamation point in the end
Does anyone see?

Does anyone care?

Stock prices up, stock prices down
Oil! We shouldn't forget that, either
Ups. And. Downs.
Wars! For these...
Can you believe?
Politicians doing poli-dicks!
Why all these
Majority believes and warships
Because it's easier
To live with.
Bubbles. Vacuum-packed lives. Unreality.
Games.
They play their games,
Make us take part
And surprise!
We are the ones
Always to lose.

ABOUT THE AUTHOR

Kurt Erkan's quest is to walk the narrow streets of the human soul. He explores our triumphs and our weaknesses, our fearless leaps and our hesitations, our attempts to become better people and our submissions to darker desires – and how every choice we make can change the paths of those around us. He is fascinated by the inner compass we all have, and how its needle can swing toward the ultimate truth when it is fed by hope.

Kurt Erkan believes that the best way to explore the inner world is by writing – namely via prose and poetry. The information discovered and riddles solved in these realms must be shared with other people who are on the same quest.

Kurt holds a BS degree in civil engineering and lives in Berlin, Germany, with his wife.

kurterkan.com | @the_taletella | taletella@hetsoff.com

HEAVEN MUST BE LIKE THIS
(Novel)

HEAVEN
MUST BE
LIKE THIS

HOPE

KURT ERKAN

HETSOFF

www.ingramcontent.com/pod-product-compliance
Lightning Source LLC
Chambersburg PA
CBHW020604030426
42337CB00013B/1208